Nine Fruits *of the* Spirit

A Bible Study on Developing Christian Character

Goodness

Robert Strand

New Leaf Press
A Division of New Leaf Publishing Group

First printing: June 1999
Third printing: September 2009

Copyright © 1999 by New Leaf Press. All rights reserved. No part
of this book may be used or reproduced in any manner whatsoever
without written permission of the publisher, except in the case of
brief quotations in articles and reviews. For information write:
New Leaf Press, P.O. Box 726, Green Forest, AR 72638.

ISBN-13: 978-0-89221-466-2
ISBN: 0-89221-466-X
Library of Congress Number: 99-64011

Cover by Janell Robertson

Printed in China

Please visit our website for other great titles:
www.newleafpress.net

For information regarding author interviews, please contact the
publicity department at (870) 438-5288.

Contents

Introduction

There is an ancient story out of the Middle East which tells of three merchants crossing the desert. They were traveling at night in the darkness to avoid the heat of the day. As they were crossing over a dry creek bed, a loud attention-demanding voice out of the darkness commanded them to stop. They were then ordered to get down off their camels, stoop down and pick up pebbles from the creek bed, and put them into their pockets.

Immediately after doing as they had been commanded, they were then told to leave that place and continue until dawn before they stopped to set up camp. This mysterious voice told them that in the morning they would be both sad and happy. Understandably shaken, they obeyed the voice and traveled on through the rest of the night without stopping. When morning dawned, these three merchants anxiously looked into their pockets. Instead of finding the pebbles as expected, there were precious jewels! And, they were both happy and sad. Happy that they had picked up some of the pebbles, but sad because they hadn't gathered more when they had the opportunity.

This fable expresses how many of us feel about the treasures of God's Word. There is coming a day when we will be thrilled because we have absorbed as much as we have, but sad because we had not gleaned much more. Jewels are best shown off when held up to a bright light and slowly turned so that each polished facet can catch and reflect the light. Each of these nine jewels of character will be examined in the light of God's Word and how best to allow them to be developed in the individual life. That is how I feel about the following three verses from Paul's writings which challenge us with what their Christian character or personality should look like. Jesus Christ has boiled down a Christian's responsibility to two succinct commands: Love the Lord your God with all your heart, mind, soul, and body, and love your neighbor like yourself. Likewise, Paul the apostle has captured for us the Christian personality in nine traits:

> But the fruit of the Spirit is love, joy, peace, patience, kindness, goodness, faithfulness, gentleness, and self-control. Against such things there is no law. Those who belong to Christ Jesus have crucified the sinful nature with its passions and desires. Since we live by the Spirit, let us keep in step with the Spirit (Gal. 5:22–25).

At the very beginning of this study, I must point out a subtle, yet obvious, distinction. The "fruit" of the Spirit is a composite description of what the Christian lifestyle and character traits are all about — an unbroken whole. We can't pick only the fruit we like.

Unlocked in these nine portraits are the riches of a Christ-centered personality. The thrill of the search is ahead of us!

Goodness

Agathos (Greek) describes that which,
a person being good in character or
constitution, will be beneficial
in its effect on others.

*THE FRUIT OF THE
SPIRIT IS . . . GOODNESS!*

"Goodness" has fallen on bad times in our day! It has a bad press connotation — after all who really wants to be "good." It's expecting people to be wimpish or weak or somehow less than

*The word agathos is
used of things which
are physical such as
a good tree (Matt.
7:17) or good ground
(Luke 8:8). It is also
used in a moral
sense of persons.
God is essentially,
absolutely, and
consummately
good. It also means
that "the good" is
morally honorable
and pleasing to God.
Christians in their
lifestyle are to prove
this to the world.
We are to be zealous
of goodness and to
overcome evil with it.*

aggressive. In the minds of too many people today, it's an old-fashioned quality which is out-of-date. We'd rather be chic, slick, popular, exciting, with it, or living on the edge.

Then . . . when you think about it, wouldn't you rather do business with a "good" merchant? Send your kids to a "good" school? Be a patient of a very "good" doctor? Drive a "good" car? Be married to a "good" spouse? Do everything you can to raise "good" kids?

"Good" and "goodness" are two very popular words in the vocabulary of our day. We like to think that what we do is "good" to benefit others. But what really is "goodness"? Are the actions of our living amounting to the greatest "good" for others?

Before we consider "being" good and "doing" good, we will be needing a working definition of goodness. The measuring rod and the standard has been set by God and not by humans. God is the measure of all things, including goodness and what it means. So we'll attempt to start with an understanding of the "goodness" of God as a harvest of the Spirit's working in our living.

> Goodness is love in action, love with its hand to the plow, love with the burden on its back, love following His footsteps who went about continually doing good.
>
> (James Hamilton)

> Wesley's Rule:
> Do all the good you can,
> By all the means you can,
> In all the ways you can,
> In all the places you can
> At all the times you can,
> To all the people you can,
> As long as ever you can.
>
> (John Wesley)

Our first study takes us to Psalm 100:1–5.

Describe what you mean by calling someone a "good" person:

_____

_____

_____

_____

Would you consider yourself a "good" person? Why? Or why not?

_____

_____

_____

_____

What do we know about the character of God from Psalm 100?

_____

_____

_____

_____

Exactly how do we know that God is good?

_____

_____

_____

_____

_____

_____

How do the actions of God reflect the goodness of God?

_____

_____

_____

_____

_____

Have you discovered how we are to worship God from this psalm?

_____

_____

_____

_____

How have you responded to the goodness of God in your life?

_____

_____

_____

_____

What do these verses say about our relationship to God?

_____

_____

_____

_____

How do we know that God is good from these passages?

_____

_____

_____

_____

_____

Relate how the goodness of God can help you with your current lifestyle:

_____

_____

_____

_____

_____

Based on what you have read in this psalm, write your working definition of goodness:

_____

_____

_____

_____

_____

_____

What do you think is meant by "his gates" and "his courts"?

_____

_____

_____

_____

_____

_____

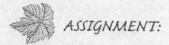 *ASSIGNMENT:*

• Consider your relationships with others. What can you do to introduce goodness into the mix?

_____

_____

_____

_____

_____

• List the things in your life which you believe are a manifestation of the goodness of God:

_____

_____

_____

_____

WHAT GOOD THING?

One of the most exciting descriptions of Jesus is found in only five words which the Apostle Peter spoke: "He went around doing good" (Acts 10:38). What an exquisite portrait! From this description, we can easily deduce what His lifestyle must have been like: He touched the lepers, He anointed the eyes of a blind man with mud, He touched little children, He healed with a touch, He personally went to the bedside of the sick, He didn't send somebody else, He did it personally.

What a lesson for us! Goodness isn't an arms-length kind of living. It is a hands-on, up-close-and-personal performance. He went about doing good without asking the cost or determining the dangers. He aggressively sought out those in need of His goodness. What an example for this generation of Christians who are seeking their own comforts, wanting to stay in their cocoons of self-satisfaction, not wanting to do the dirty work of people contacts — but depending on others to do their good works for them by simply "paying" their dues and giving monetary means so others can be sent. Just because we don't want to be in the touching business doesn't exempt us from this work of doing good to others wherever we find a need.

Charles Colson tells us about a prison riot which took place in Washington, DC's Lorton prison complex. Inmates were on the rampage . . . torching buildings with armed gangs roaming the grounds to do any damage they could. But in the main prison exercise yard, there was a group of Christian inmates standing in a huge circle, arms linked together, and singing hymns. Inside this circle was a group of prison guards and other prisoners who were seeking protection from the rioting inmates.[1]

What a sharp contrast is drawn in this story. This is the kind of distinction we as Christians must draw in a dark world. Jesus said that we are to be the "light of the world" in contrast to the darkness of this worldly system. Contrast is what this

You know what has happened throughout Judea . . . how God anointed Jesus of Nazareth with the Holy Spirit and power, and how he went around doing good and healing all who were under the power of the devil, because God was with him (Acts 10:37–38).

is all about! What is it that can draw this sharp contrast between a Christian and the world about him/her?

Our next study takes us to a young man and an interesting question which has implications for today. Please read Matthew 19:16–30 and then come back to work our way through these study questions:

Is it possible to do a "good thing" to earn eternal life?

_____

_____

_____

To whom did Jesus refer to as being "good" and why?

_____

_____

_____

_____

Why did Jesus list only six of the Ten Commandments?

_____

_____

_____

_____

_____

Is it enough to keep the commandments to gain eternal life?
Explain:

_____

_____

_____

_____

_____

In verse 21, why did Jesus zero in on the young man's earthly possessions?

_____

_____

_____

From verse 23, why is it so hard for rich people to enter the kingdom of heaven?

_____

_____

_____

_____

Is getting rid of all your earthly possessions still a requirement to be able to enter the kingdom of heaven?

_____

_____

_____

How can you answer the disciples' question: "Who then can be saved?"

_____

_____

_____

_____

_____

_____

Please explain the analogy of a "camel" and the "eye of the needle":

_____

_____

_____

_____

_____

_____

What special reward did Jesus speak about to and for the 12 disciples?

_____

_____

_____

_____

In the bottom line, does "goodness" really have anything to do with entering the kingdom of heaven?

_____

_____

_____

Verse 29 begins with an inclusive, "And everyone. . . . " How does this apply to you?

_____

_____

_____

What does verse 30 have to do with goodness and how is it to be worked out in daily living?

_____

_____

_____

_____

_____

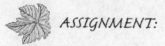 ASSIGNMENT:

• How does "giving to the poor" relate to goodness?

_____

_____

_____

_____

_____

_____

• Whom do you know that you can help and minister goodness to?

_____

_____

_____

_____

_____

Specifically, what life actions will you plan to do?

_____

_____

_____

_____

_____

_____

_____

A GOOD KING IN ACTION

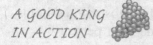

The supreme test of goodness is not in the greater but in the smaller incidents of our character and practice; not what we are when standing in the searchlight of public scrutiny, but when we reach the firelight flicker of our homes; not what we are when some clarion call rings through the air, summoning us to fight for life and liberty, but our attitude when we are called to sentry-duty in the gray morning, when the watch-fire is burning low. It is impossible to be our best at the supreme moment if character is corroded and eaten into by daily inconsistency, unfaithfulness, and besetting sin. (F.B. Meyer)

For the Lord is good and his love endures forever; his faithfulness continues through all generations (Ps. 100:5).

Goodness may be best understood when it is painted boldly in the life actions of another person. One such person was an Old Testament king named Josiah. What is so interesting in this study is the fact that he became a king at age 8! How many 8 year olds do you know who are capable of leading a nation? It also indicates that while still a teenager, age 16, "he began to seek the God of his father David."

Let's read the account from 2 Chronicles 34:1–7; 14–33.

Who was Josiah and how did he become king at the ripe old age of 8?

_____

_____

_____

_____

_____

_____

_____

Verse 2 says all we really need to know about this king. What do you think were his life actions that caused the writer to record such a compliment?

_____

_____

_____

_____

_____

What was it that needed to be purged from his nation?

_____

_____

_____

_____

_____

What was an "Asherah pole"?

_____

_____

_____

_____

_____

_____

What was the significance of the "altars of Baal"?

_____

_____

_____

_____

_____

_____

_____

From verse 14, what was so significant about finding the "Book of the Law of the Lord"?

_____

_____

_____

_____

What caused the king to tear his robes?

_____

_____

_____

What is the relationship between the Word of God and goodness in action?

_____

_____

_____

_____

What was it that would bring the judgment of God and curses down upon the Israelites?

_____

_____

_____

_____

How was this judgment averted?

_____

_____

_____

_____

Explain what a "covenant" is (verse 31) and why it needed to be renewed?

_____

_____

_____

_____

Why would you consider the example of Josiah an example of goodness in action?

_____

_____

_____

_____

ASSIGNMENT:

• What is there about our world that may be parallel to the life and times of Josiah?

_____

_____

_____

_____

_____

• Exactly how can goodness be brought to bear on modern-day problems?

_____

_____

_____

_____

_____

_____

What can you do specifically to help our world system experience a turnabout?

_____

_____

_____

_____

_____

_____

THE STRUGGLE BETWEEN GOOD AND EVIL

Being good and exhibiting goodness may be a battleground. Just because you decide to let goodness become a part of your lifestyle doesn't necessarily mean that it will happen without a struggle.

In his book, *How to Begin the Christian Life*, George Sweeting tells this story: "In an Italian city stands a statue of a Grecian maiden with a beautiful face, a graceful figure, and a noble expression. One day a poor little peasant girl came face to face with the statue. She stood and stared and then went home to wash her face and comb her hair. The next day she came again to stand before the statue and then to return home once more. This time she mended her tattered clothing. Day by day she changed, her form grew more graceful, and her face more refined,

Do not be overcome by evil, but overcome evil with good (Rom. 12:21).

until she greatly reflected the famous statue. She was transformed in appearance!"[2]

Just so, the committed Christian must every day in every way seek to conform to the perfect image of Jesus Christ. This growing in goodness is not a once-for-all kind of experience.

I remind you once more that fruit is something that grows under the cultivation of the Spirit in your life. It's a process, a daily commitment, a daily discipline, a daily application of the biblical truth. Every day, in some small and sometimes very significant way, we should all be changing into His likeness.

But the reality is that progress isn't a steady kind of thing. There are ups and downs, good days and bad days, good and evil are a constant struggle. Many of us can identify with the struggle as expressed by the writer Paul, "For I have the desire to do what is good, but I cannot carry it out!" (Rom. 7:18). What a dilemma and what a struggle! How is it possible for the human being to experience good overcoming evil?

For this particular study, begin by reading Romans 7:14–8:8; 12:9, 21.

What is there about human nature that you can understand from these passages?

_____

_____

_____

_____

Where is this battleground for the fight between good and evil taking place?

_____

_____

_____

Do you see yourself relating to Paul's struggle? If so, please explain:

_____

_____

_____

_____

What does Paul identify as the enemy to doing good?

_____

_____

_____

What happens at the point of doing good?

_____

_____

_____

_____

How do YOU handle this tension between good and evil that Paul describes?

_____

_____

_____

_____

How does this inner struggle affect your ability to live a life filled with goodness?

_____

_____

_____

_____

_____

_____

How are we set free from this struggle?

_____

_____

_____

_____

_____

_____

From verses 8:5–8, explain what the "mind controlled by the Spirit" is in real living:

_____

_____

_____

_____

In Romans 12:9 and 21, what is Paul attempting to say to you?

_____

_____

_____

What are some of the evils in our society which need to be overcome by good?

_____

_____

_____

_____

What part is the Spirit playing in your life in the development of goodness?

_____

_____

_____

_____

_____

 ASSIGNMENT:

• In your own life, give an example of what it means to cling to the good in the midst of what may be evil:

_____

_____

_____

_____

_____

_____

• Specifically, what are you doing to overcome evil in any of your relationships?

_____

_____

_____

_____

_____

_____

List areas in your life where you are experiencing victories in overcoming evil:

_____

_____

_____

_____

_____

_____

THE "GOOD" LIFESTYLE

Duffy Daugherty, former football coach at Michigan State University, tells of Dave Kaiser's winning field goal in a game against UCLA. The game was played in Los Angeles and the field goal gave State a last-second 17 to 14 victory. As Dave came back to the bench to meet the roaring enthusiasm of his teammates, Coach Daugherty said: "Nice going, Dave, but I noticed you didn't watch the ball after you kicked it. How come?"

Kaiser replied, "You are right Coach, I didn't watch the ball. I was watching the referee to see how he would call it. You see, I forgot my contact lenses. They are back at the hotel. I couldn't even see the goal posts!"

You are the light of the world. A city on a hill cannot be hidden. Neither do people light a lamp and put it under a bowl. Instead they put it on its stand, and it gives light to everyone in the house. In the same way, let your light shine before men, that they may see your good deeds and praise your Father in heaven (Matt. 5:14–16).

Coach Daugherty was shocked and at first quite angry that Kaiser had not told him about the missing contacts. But after he thought it over he changed his mind. Why shouldn't Kaiser kick without his contacts? He was a disciplined kicker and had practiced long hours. He knew well the angle and the distance to the goal even though he could not see it. The whole process of kicking the ball was programmed into his body and mind by the ongoing discipline of daily practice. In that moment when the ball went through the uprights, discipline paid off.

In a similar sense, our Christian behavior can be habitual and even automatic. Discipline is one of our most effective ways for guiding our actions in a positive sense. If we learn something right the first time and continue to practice it . . . we can be counted on to do it right when the pressure is on, even when the odds may be against us. Daily discipline and perseverance in practice are still the pathway to maturing in goodness of character. The Holy Spirit of God is the active agent in this process. We put in the Word, discipline ourselves, and the Spirit nurtures the ongoing living of it in practice.

THE BEATITUDES
Blessed are the poor in spirit,
for theirs is the kingdom of heaven.

Blessed are those who mourn,
    for they will be comforted.
Blessed are the meek,
    for they will inherit the earth.
Blessed are those who hunger and thirst for
    righteousness, for they will be filled.
Blessed are the merciful,
    for they will be shown mercy.
Blessed are the pure in heart,
    for they will see God.
Blessed are the peacemakers,
    for they will be called sons of God.
Blessed are those who are persecuted
    because of righteousness,
    for theirs is the kingdom of heaven.

Blessed are you when people insult you, persecute you and falsely say all kinds of evil against you because of me. Rejoice and be glad, because great is your reward in heaven, for in the same way they persecuted the prophets who were before you (Matt. 5:3–11).

So what does the "good" lifestyle really look like? I'm so glad that has already been answered by our road map for living, the

Bible. There is a section that is one of the most famous of all the biblical passages in which the good life is outlined for all of us to read and put into action.

For this final wrap-up study, let's read it from the "Sermon on the Mount" in which Jesus captured the good life for all of us for all time, Matthew 5:1–48.

To whom is Jesus teaching these truths?

_____

_____

_____

What does it mean to be "blessed"?

_____

_____

_____

_____

_____

_____

What life actions is Jesus suggesting in His listing of the Beatitudes?

_____

_____

_____

_____

_____

_____

_____

_____

_____

_____

If we learn something right the first time and continue to practice it . . . we can be counted on to do it right when the pressure is on, even when the odds may be against us. Daily discipline and perseverance in practice are still the pathway to maturing in goodness of character.

From verse 13, what does it mean to be "the salt of the earth"?

_____

_____

_____

_____

_____

_____

From verse 14, what does it mean to be "the light of the world"?

_____

_____

_____

_____

_____

_____

How does being "salt" and "light" relate specifically to goodness?

_____

_____

_____

_____

_____

Who receives the glory when we are letting our "light shine before" others? Why?

_____

_____

_____

_____

_____

How are difficult "matters" (verse 25) to be settled between Christians?

_____

_____

_____

_____

_____

_____

How can you relate goodness in relationship to adultery and divorce?

_____

_____

_____

_____

_____

_____

In the Old Testament, actions were punishable by death . . . but here in this sermon, Jesus talks about thought patterns. How does goodness relate to our thinking the right kinds of thoughts?

_____

_____

_____

_____

_____

From verses 43–47, how can you turn an enemy into a friend?

_____

_____

_____

_____

_____

_____

What do you think it means to "be perfect . . . as your heavenly Father is perfect?"

_____

_____

_____

_____

_____

How can anybody be perfect?

_____

_____

_____

_____

_____

_____

Or is it just possible Jesus is talking about "maturity" rather than "perfection" in our understanding? Explain:

_____

_____

_____

_____

_____

If goodness is a character trait you might be a bit short on . . . how are you planning to move into a lifestyle marked by goodness?

_____

_____

_____

_____

_____

_____

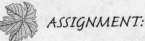 *ASSIGNMENT:*

• After working our way through these studies, how does God's goodness determine the meaning of ultimate good?

_____

_____

_____

_____

_____

• Specifically, what steps are you willing to take to implement a life of goodness which is pleasing to God?

_____

_____

_____

_____

_____

THE GOODNESS CREED

Let me be a little kinder,
Let me be a little blinder
To the faults of those about me;
Let me praise a little more;
Let me be, when I am weary,
Just a little bit more cheery;
Think a little more of others
And a little less of me.

Let me be a little braver
When temptation bids me waver;
Let me strive a little harder
To be all that I should be.

Let me be a little meeker
With the brother who is weaker;
Let me think more of my neighbor
And a little less of me.

Let me be when I am weary
Just a little bit more cheery
Let me serve a little better
Those that I am striving for.

Let me be a little sweeter,
Make my life a bit completer,
By doing what I should do
Every minute of the day.

Let me toil without complaining,
Not a humble task disdaining;
Let me face the summons calmly
When death beckons me away.

(Author is unknown)

Living the "good" life should be one of our highest goals in life. When we are at our best, we are the most effective in living. This good life, as we have discovered, is not some wimpish kind of existence . . . but a life filled with the highest callings and highest values. This good life is a very real possibility for all of us!

You can have the good life — a life of goodness for others, a harvest of fruit for the bettering of others. This life is not dependent upon what the world considers to be a good life — the right beer, the right cigarette, the right car, the right deodorant, having the right mate, or living in the right house! The life of goodness is a life with God at the center. It's a lifestyle which recognizes that God has placed within each of us the potential of goodness which can be lived every day. We cannot be at our best until we allow the Spirit of God to work within us so that Jesus Christ living through us can touch this world with goodness!

> Make a tree good and its fruit will be good, or make a tree bad and its fruit will be bad, for a tree is recognized by its fruit. . . . For out of the overflow of the heart the mouth speaks. The GOOD

God has placed within each of us the potential of goodness which can be lived every day.

man brings GOOD things out of the GOOD stored up in him, and the evil man brings evil things out of the evil stored up in him (Matt. 12:33–35).

DO NOT BE OVERCOME BY EVIL, BUT OVERCOME EVIL WITH GOOD!

And the fruit of the Spirit is . . . GOODNESS!

1 Charles Colson, *Against the Night* (Ann Arbor, MI: Vine Books, 1991), adapted.
2 George Sweeting, *How to Begin the Christian Life* (Chicago, IL: Moody Press, 1993).

Nine Fruits of the Spirit

Study Series includes

Love

Joy

Peace

Patience

Kindness

Goodness

Faithfulness

Gentleness

Self-Control

Robert Strand

Retired from a 40-year ministry career with the Assemblies of God, this "pastor's pastor" is adding to his reputation as a prolific author. The creator of the fabulously successful Moments to Give series (over one million in print), Strand travels extensively, gathering research for his books and mentoring pastors. He and his wife, Donna, live in Springfield, Missouri. They have four children.

Rev. Strand is a graduate of North Central Bible College with a degree in theology.